Other books in this series:
Thank Heavens for Friends   For My Father
For Mother, a Gift of Love   Marriage a Keepsake
Love a Celebration   To My Daughter With Love

EDITED BY HELEN EXLEY
BORDER ILLUSTRATIONS BY SHARON BASSIN

Published simultaneously in 1994 by Exley Publications in
Great Britain, and Exley Giftbooks in the USA.

12 11 10 9 8 7 6 5 4 3

ISBN 1-85015-452-X

A copy of the CIP data is available from the British Library
on request.

Designed by Pinpoint Design.
Picture research by P. A. Goldberg and J. Clift/Image Select.
Typeset by Delta, Watford.
Printed and bound by Grafo, S.A., Bilbao, Spain.

Exley Publications Ltd, 16 Chalk Hill, Watford,
Herts WD1 4BN, United Kingdom.
Exley Giftbooks, 232 Madison Avenue, Suite 1206,
NY 10016, USA.

To my
GRANDMOTHER
with love

EDITED BY
HELEN EXLEY

NEW YORK • WATFORD, UK

Grandmas sometimes race you to the next lamp post ... but then they sit on a wall and turn a funny shade.

The most maddening thing about grandmas is that they don't *use* the gifts you give them. They even keep the ribbon.

Grandmas don't just say "that's nice" - they reel back and roll their eyes and throw up their hands and smile. You get your money's worth out of grandmas.

It takes a lifetime to get back to knowing you don't know anything: that's why grandmothers and grandchildren get on so well together.

Of course, there *are* grandmas that believe in Clean Clothes and Sitting Up To Table - but they don't get asked round too often.

It is remarkable how, overnight, a fat, elderly lady can learn to sit cross legged on the floor and play a tin drum, quack like a duck, sing all the verses of "The Twelve Days of Christmas", make paper flowers, draw pigs and sew on the ears of severely injured teddy bears.

Grandmothers walk slowly and so rediscover petrol rainbows, fallen leaves, puddles and worms in need of rescue.

Grandmothers have old feet and young hearts.

Grandmas are *always* astonished to find themselves old enough to be grandmas.

In their bags grandmas have peppermints, toilet paper, aspirin, scissors, needle and thread, scotch tape, Band-aids, a police whistle, three combs, six ballpoints and a pencil, a penknife, a spoon, a clump of safety pins, another bag of peppermints, a length of string, four elastic bands, a diary, an address book, a pack of postcards, six stamps with no sticky, a tube of paper paste and an Agatha Christie.

Some mothers are very ambitious for their children. Most grandmas just want the children to be happy – they've discovered for themselves just how little time everyone has.

WHAT IS A GRANDMOTHER?

A grandmother is a lady who has no children of her own, so she likes other people's little girls and boys. A grandfather is a man grandmother. He goes for walks with the boys and they talk about fishing and tractors.

Grandmothers don't have to do anything but be there. They are old so they shouldn't play hard or run. They should never say, "Hurry up". Usually they are fat, but not too fat to tie children's shoes.

They wear glasses and funny underwear, and they can take their teeth and gums off.

They don't have to be smart, only answer questions, like why dogs hate cats and why God isn't married. They don't talk baby-talk like visitors. When they read to us, they don't skip bits, or mind if it is the same story over again.

Everybody should have one, especially if you don't have television, because grandmothers are the only grown-ups who have the time!

PATSY GRAY, AGED 7

There's something engaging
about the combination of very young people
and very mature people.
A child challenges most parents
to be stable and responsible.
A grandchild challenges the grandparent
to put aside all that stuff
and have fun.

CHARLES AND ANN MORSE

The oddities of shape that age has given me,
defeating exercise and diet,
making me appear hump-backed, pot-bellied,
  flabby-armed
when inside in reality I am slim and straight
and, bracing all my muscles,
prove to be purpose-built
for carting grandchildren from place to place.
I am a breathing, ambulatory armchair
the perfect place for cuddles.

PAM BROWN

A good granny clucks over your carry-cot the minute you're born and says: "Well, I never did. This is the most beautiful baby I've ever seen in my life - and I'm not prejudiced."...

When you make her an Easter card at nursery school, she keeps it in her handbag and fishes it out to show her friends, and the nice woman standing beside her in the bus queue.

Then she sticks it in a scrapbook, together with one of your baby curls, and an item in the local paper announcing that you came third in the fancy-dress competition organized by the Junior Chamber of Commerce.

When you're top of the class, she gives you a quid and a kiss and tells everyone: "You wouldn't think that anyone as clever as my little granddaughter could be so beautiful, too."

But if your school report says, "Must try harder," she says: "Never mind, ducks. Look at Winston Churchill. He never did himself justice at school, and neither did your Uncle Fred - and look where he is now. If you want my opinion, those clever dicks who pass exams burn themselves out before they've begun - and that's a fact."

When your Mum says, "What do you think you're playing at sitting down at the table with a mucky face," your granny murmurs: "It's only *clean* dirt."

When your Dad takes one look at your lurex ankle socks and Afghan jerkin and says, "You're not going out like that, are you?" your granny says: "Well I think she looks a picture."

And, on your wedding day, she takes your brand-new husband aside, puts a little wrinkled hand on his arm and hisses in his ear: "You're a very lucky lad. That girl could have had her pick, you know."

Even though it was you who had your work cut out catching *him*.

PENNY PERRICK

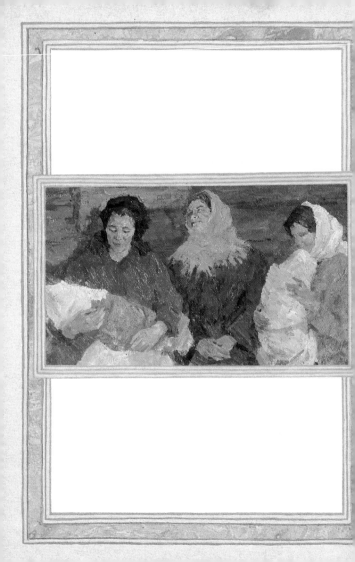

Who went into mild hysterics when told the
  news?
Who suffered nine months of waiting,
  wondering and secretly agonising?
Who waited for twelve hours by the phone
  waiting for news?
Who rushed off to the hospital babbling like an
  idiot?
Who bawled like a baby when shown him?
Who's the proudest and daftest person when
  he's around?
Who shows him off like some priceless jewel?
Who? Me, Mark's very lucky grandma.

L. MILNES

I had forgotten how beautiful a newborn baby is. It is a myth that all babies look alike. Some newborn babies are red and scrawny and squally; others are pink and cuddly and cute. I suppose you think that, as a grandmother, I might be prejudiced about this particular baby, but my years as a journalist have made it possible for me to observe objectively, and in so doing, I have to admit that Joshua Lee Bloomingdale, at age fifty-three minutes, was the most beautiful baby God ever created.

TERESA BLOOMINGDALE

My baby daughter arrived, and brought with her – immortality! No longer was I one person. I was two persons, with the glorious possibility of being a part of any number of persons in the future.

My ideas; my moral standards; my oddities and idiosyncrasies; my love of books and games; my horror of mice; my inability to do the simplest sums; the awkward surge of emotion that overcomes me when I see human goodness - some part of me had a chance of living after me, and even spreading - so that there might be a bit of me in the world for a long time to come! I liked the idea.

It may sound a bit self-satisfied, but I hope my daughter and now my beloved granddaughter, "the pulse and core of my heart", (as the Irish say) have not learned or inherited anything really *bad* from me. I may have spoiled them a bit, but only with love, and I don't believe *real* love does any harm. (Real love can be very tough.) And how bare my life would have been without them. I'm an old woman now, and can go off happily into the unknown sure that there's a lot of me left behind.

EMILY WORTHINGTON

WHAT IS A GRANDMOTHER?

A grandmother is a little girl who suddenly shows up one day with a touch of grey in her hair.

Better than anything, she has a way of understanding little boys. Especially men who are grown-up little boys.

Something about a grandmother is always making you hungry. Maybe it's the apple pies baking and the chicken frying and the biscuits in the oven. But Grandma always has the nicest smelling house.

Long before Band-Aids were invented, she was the best person to take care of scraped knees and scratched elbows and banged heads. It was something in the way she touched you.

Grandmother was an expert on mischief, too. Especially when you had been into it. When she looked right into your eyes it was pretty hard to fool her about what really happened. Really.

And it was when you were almost too big to sit in her lap that you began to learn that she was a very special person to talk to. Sometimes, she would give you the right answers without ever saying a word.

HARRY McMAHAN

Get up! Get washed! Eat your breakfast!
That's my mum,
Going on and on and on and on and on . . .

Sit down! Shut up!
Get on with your work! !
That's my teacher,
Going on and on and on and on and on . . .

Come here! Give me that!
That's my big sister,
Going on and on and on and on and on . . .

Get off! Stop it! Carry me!
That's my little sister,
Going on and on and on and on and on . . .

Boss. Boss. Boss
They do it all day.
Sometimes I think I'll run away,
But I don't know
Where to go.

The only one who doesn't do it,
Is my old gran.
She says, "Would you like to get washed?"
Or, "Would you like to sit on this chair?"
And she listens to what I say.

People say she spoils me,
And that she's old-fashioned.
I think it's the others that spoil;
Spoil every day.
And I wish more people were old-fashioned,
. . . like my gran.

JOHN CUNLIFFE

I know a little cupboard
With a teeny tiny key
And there's a jar of Lollipops
  For me, me, me.

It has a little shelf, my dear,
As dark as dark can be,
And there's a dish of Banbury Cakes
  For me, me, me.

I have a small fat grandmama
With a very slippery knee,
And she's Keeper of the Cupboard
   With the key, key, key.

And when I'm very good, my dear,
As good as good can be
There's Banbury Cakes, and Lollipops
   For me, me, me.

WALTER DE LA MARE

GRANDMA COMES WEDNESDAYS

Grandma comes dragged down with bags,
hair all awry,
Clean out of breath from puffing up the road.
She sits and sags
till Mum has stoked her up with tea,
and I sit on her knee
and struggle not to pry
into that interesting load
until she gives the word.
One bulge is bound to be for me
for Mum gets food
and Dad gets two or three
posh motor magazines
she's given where she cleans,
but I get special things
like buttons, shiny beads,
bottles that smell of scent,
a bird
all stuck with sequins,
rings
with diamonds big as peas,
and, once, a bear
that, as Grandma says,
has personality -
and seeds
to sow behind the garden shed.

She brings nice goodies
does my Gran
And likes to come to see
my rabbit
and the frog I found that's dead
and stays
to read a story
when I go to bed.

PAM BROWN

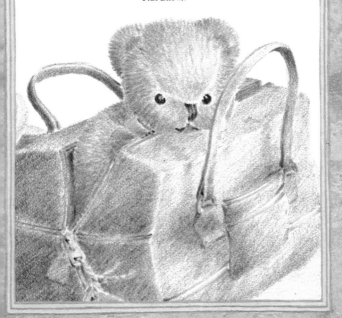

GRANDMA GOES TO A PARTY

I would unzip my skin
and hang it on a chair,
take off this wig,
let down my yellow hair
and dance until the dawn
. . . if I could break the spell
that trickster time has played.
But all the words are lost.
This wearisome charade
must go on as before.
I watch the children spin.
And sigh. And yawn.

PAM BROWN

BABBLING AND GABBLING

My Granny's an absolute corker,
My Granny's an absolute cracker,
But she's Britain's speediest talker
And champion yackety-yacker!

Everyone's fond of my Granny,
Everyone thinks she's nice,
But before you can say Jack Robinson,
My Granny's said it twice!

KIT WRIGHT

In love with his neighbour's daughter, Mr. Dorsun Yilmaz of Dalmali, Yugoslavia, organized an elopement.

Soon after midnight, his beloved, wrapped in a blanket, descended the ladder he had placed by her window. He carried her to the car and away they sped.

Five miles down the road he unwrapped his treasure, and found that he was carrying the girl's grandmother, who beat him up.

"THE SUN", AUGUST 26, 1972

The odd antics of merry widow Jennie Gorman have got her barred from a nightclub.

For right in the middle of a comedy act at the club, she got up from the audience and insisted on showing off her dancing outfit. She unzipped her purple evening gown to reveal red hot pants, fishnet stockings and garters. And emblazoned on her chest was a saucy "I'm A Virgin" badge.

It was all too much for Derek Kirkbride, manager of the club, the Rendezvous in Workington, Cumberland. He reckoned that Jennie had gone too far - it was no way for a *seventy-four*-year-old granny to behave.

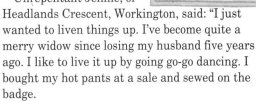

He said: "It wasn't the sort of display we want in this club. I told her never to come in here again. She is known in another club in the town for go-go dancing in her hot pants, but she's never dared to do it in our place before."

Unrepentant Jennie, of Headlands Crescent, Workington, said: "I just wanted to liven things up. I've become quite a merry widow since losing my husband five years ago. I like to live it up by going go-go dancing. I bought my hot pants at a sale and sewed on the badge.

"Too old at 74? Not a bit of it. I'm just beginning to live."

SYDNEY FOXCROFT,
FROM A NEWSCUTTING IN THE "SUNDAY PEOPLE"

OLD MRS. BODFAN'S DANCE

Oh! Crikey. O, Oh! Crikey-O,
I smell the spring today.
I smell the earth,
I hear buds burst,
I feel the roots begin to stir.
The birds are singing in the hedge
and soft air turns my vane.
Everywhere I look are signs
that spring is here again.

Oh! Crikey-O, Oh! Crikey-O,
no spring is in my bones
not in my face,
not in my hair,
not in my step or stoop.
Yet I must give a *little* leap
in welcome to the spring,
and thank the Lord who's let me live
to see this season in.

KUSHA PETTS

GRANDMOTHER EXTRAORDINARY

Her exploits excited a variety of reactions among family and friends at home. Attitudes ranged from admiration to incredulity, amazement was mixed with amused tolerance. But from one generation of the Nicholl family she knew only unreserved affection, tinged with adulation. Her grandchildren were devoted to her. She, who as a young mother had felt a certain estrangement from her own children, discovered in her grandchildren a never-ending source of pleasure. And they, in their turn, adored her. For Grandmama knew so much about everything. From her they learnt the names of the flowers and trees, how to identify the birds and the butterflies, and country walks with Grandmama were a constant delight. And unlike most grown-ups she was an enthusiastic supporter of such activities as tree-climbing and rock-climbing, her own pleasure rivalling that of her grandchildren when any of them showed the same fearless courage and instinctive climbing prowess that she herself had possessed. And then there was Grandmama's marvellous repertoire of stories that never palled in the repeated telling, tales of her own adventures and tales of her imagination that held her young audience spell-bound.

It is in the memories of her grandchildren that Mary De la Beche Nicholl still lives today. Some were fortunate enough to accompany Grandmama on her travels, and have left their own descriptions of the events of those travels. Gwennie (later Lyon) went with her grandmother to the Gredos Mountains of Spain and experienced at first hand the adventure of tents, camps under the stars, donkey and horse rides, and the inevitable butterfly hunts. Members of the Nicholl family still recall with amused affection a letter from Gwennie describing her Spanish travels and recounting how Grandmama was received by the mayor and band of one remote Spanish village and conducted with great ceremony to the town hall. Minnie had been mistaken for Queen Victoria! And there are other grandchildren alive today who can still recall with unclouded memory and unreserved affection the fascinating person who was Grandmama.

HILARY M. THOMAS, FROM "GRANDMOTHER EXTRAORDINARY"

WHEN I LOOK IN YOUR EYES

This is my favourite song – of all the ones I sing.
I think of my grandmother whenever I sing it.

FRANKIE VAUGHAN

When I look in your eyes
I see the wisdom of the world in your eyes,
I see the sadness of a thousand goodbyes
When I look in your eyes
. . . Autumn comes, summer dies,
I see the passing of the years in your eyes,
And when we part there'll be no tears, no
    goodbyes,
I'll just look into your eyes.
Those eyes so wise, so warm, so real,
How I love the world your eyes reveal.

LESLIE BRICUSSE

TENDER LOVING CARE

My granddaughter is two and takes good care
   of me,
gives me the spectacles I just took off,
insists I drink the abandoned cup of tea,
fetches her linctus for my smoker's cough,
runs in to get the book I meant to leave behind,
orders me off to have an after dinner nap.
She's loving, thoughtful, orderly and kind.
God help her husband, poor beloved chap.

PAM BROWN

GRANDCHILD

She stumbles upon every day
as though it were a four-leaf clover
ringed in a horseshoe.

The light is her luck – and its thickening
into chair, postman, poodle
with a ribbon round its neck.

She plays among godsends
and becomes one. Watch her being
a seal or a sleepy book.

Yet sometimes she wakes in the night
terrified, staring
at somewhere else.

She's learning that ancestors
refuse to be dead. Their resurrection
is her terror.

We soothe the little godsend
back to us
and pray, despairingly –

May the clover be
a true prophet. May her light be
without history.

Norman MacCaig

LOOKING BACK

After I reached the age of fourteen, my grandmother's intellectual limitations became trying to me, and her Puritan morality began to seem to me to be excessive; but while I was a child her great affection for me, and her intense care for my welfare, made me love her and gave me that feeling of safety that children need. I remember when I was about four or five years old lying awake thinking how dreadful it would be when my grandmother was dead. When she did in fact die, which was after I was married, I did not mind at all. But in retrospect, as I have grown older, I have realized more and more the importance she had in moulding my outlook on life. Her fearlessness, her public spirit, her contempt for convention, and her indifference to the opinion of the majority have always seemed good to me and have impressed themselves upon me as worthy of imitation.

BERTRAND RUSSELL

COWSLIPS

After primroses, cowslips;
I like the name.
Born overnight in open fields
with new grass, first buttercups;
friends of the clay, they have a secret look.
Their heads catch the sun's gold,
dew pearls roll among crinkled leaves,
bees dust probing tongues in honeyed tubes.

My grandmother loved these flowers,
her mother, too, with the long apron strings,
gathered bunches in these same fields
for winter wine, syrups and creams;
I inherit them now, pick a hundred at a time,
make them into tight balls, as they did,
cowslip balls to hang about the thatched house,
smelling of orange and lemon,
pomanders in spring.

LEONARD CLARK

To become a grandmother is to be suddenly piercingly aware of the brevity of human life. Only the day before yesterday and I was trailing behind my parents, poking in ditches, chivvying ants, calling "Wait for me!"

Only yesterday I came home in the clapped-out Morris, a shawl-swathed wrinkled red face in the crook of my arm, puckered against the unfamiliar sky.

And now, here is a face so like that other - but another generation, another step into unknown centuries.

That young couple I trotted behind have walked away into shadow. I recall them so vividly that it seems impossible I cannot share this new child with them - and I relive their loss. As they must have yearned for their lost and recollected parents when I myself was born, and my children in their turn.

We are old. We are young. The child, still calling "Wait for me!" touches for a little while the life of this other child. How strange that it should think me old, should even call me Grandmother.

How strange that this small, helpless thing will stand one day, astonishingly soon, where I now stand, and wonder where those past, bright summers went. As every grandma has since time began.

Every generation whispers its urgent message in the children's ears - "Treasure every moment. Learn. Live. Create. Reach out your arms. Look about you. You have so little time." And every child smiles - for it knows it has all time at its disposal and that it will not, cannot, fail.

CHARLOTTE GRAY

IN MEMORY OF MAINIE JELLETT

You died the year that I was born
and so I claim no more than kinship;
yet this sketch in oils - some corn-stooks,
sea, the hills, the shallow glow
of threatened sunlight sixty years
ago: I saw these only yesterday
in this same place; the sheaves
(still sheaves) still gathered in by hand
and fed entire to the beasts - this sketch

brings you alive, perhaps as you were then,
intense as that blue band of sea.
Were your tears then more salt,
or did your blood run wild and brackish
as the sea runs in the Hebrides,
and was this painting how you smoothed
such troubled waters?
　Fresh on this board
and through your eye in mine
they glisten still.

JOHN PURSER

OLD WOMAN

So much she caused she cannot now account for
As she stands watching day return, the cool
Walls of the house moving towards the sun.
She puts some flowers in a vase and thinks
    "There is not much I can arrange
In here and now, but flowers are suppliant

As children never were. And love is now
A flicker of memory, my body is
My own entirely. When I lie at night
I gather nothing now into my arms,
    No child or man, and where I live
Is what remains when men and children go."

Yet she owns more than residue of lives
That she has marked and altered. See how she
Warns time from too much touching her
   possessions
   By keeping flowers fed by polishing
    Her fine old silver. Gratefully
She sees her own glance printed on
   grandchildren.

Drawing the curtains back and opening
    windows
Every morning now, she feels her years
Grow less and less. Time puts no burden on
Her now she does not need to measure it.
    It is acceptance she arranges
And her own life she places in the vase.

ELIZABETH JENNINGS

Grandparents are to be thanked
for changing a child's fear of old age
into a thing of strange beauty.
It happens with the grandparent
who gives a child tasty things to eat
or who shows the child old and worn treasures
or who knows how to touch a child as he
  awakens.
Grandparents are to be thanked
for showing a child,
at the beginning of life,
the gentleness of the end of life.

A parent can give a child the stuff of reality;
but a grandparent can clothe that reality
with feelings which make it desirable.
A grandparent's special vision
may not be to see a new world.
But he can know that the old world was good.
And in himself he can reconcile the old and the
  new.
That is a vision worth sharing.

Grandparents will be thanked
for what they have spoken
and for what they have kept to themselves.
The discoveries they have kept silent about,
leaving the child to find his own.

The dreams, the mistakes, the doubts,
the worries, and the fears of old age
they share only carefully with the young.

Yet without these burdens shared,
none has a chance to grow old gracefully.
Grandparents are to be thanked
for trying anything new,
for the courage to retire
and begin again.

CHARLES AND ANN MORSE

I CAN ANSWER "YES"

July 5th, 1868: Today I have completed sixty-four Springtimes . . . And now here I am, a very old woman, embarked on my sixty-fifth year. By one of those strange oddities in my destiny, I am now in much better health, much stronger, much more active, than I ever was in my youth.... I am troubled by no hankering after the days of my youth: I am no longer ambitious for fame: I desire no money except insofar as I should like to be able to leave something to my children and grandchildren.... This astonishing old age ... has brought me neither infirmity nor lowered vitality.

Can I still make myself useful? That one may legitimately ask, and I think that I can answer "yes". I feel that I may be useful in a more personal, more direct way than ever before. I have, though how I do not know, acquired much wisdom. I am better equipped to bring up children.... It is quite wrong to think of old age as a downward slope. One climbs higher and higher with the advancing years, and that, too, with surprising strides.

How good life is when all that one loves is aswarm with life!

GEORGE SAND, FROM A LETTER TO A FRIEND

ACKNOWLEDGEMENTS: The publishers gratefully acknowledge permission to reproduce copyright material. Every effort has been made to trace copyright holders, but in a few cases this has proved impossible. The publishers would be interested to hear from any copyright holders not here acknowledged. HILAIRE BELLOC, "Grandmama's Birthday" reprinted by permission of the Peters Faser & Dunlop Group Ltd.; TERESA BLOOMINGDALE, excerpt from *Murphy Must Have Been a Mother.* Copyright © 1982 by Teresa Bloomingdale. Used by permission of Doubleday, a division of Bantam Doubleday Dell Publishing Group, Inc.; LESLIE BRICUSSE, "When I look in your eyes" from *Doctor Dolittle.* © 1967 EMI Hastings catalog/EMI catalog partnership. Reprinted by permission of C.P.P/Belwin Europe, Surrey, England. PAM BROWN, "Grandma comes Wednesdays", "Grandma goes to a party" and "Tender loving care" © Pam Brown 1983; LEONARD CLARK, "Cowslips" from *Collected Poems and Veses for Children,* published by Dobson Books Ltd.; JOHN CUNLIFFE, "Orders of the Day" from *2nd Poetry Book,* compiled by John Foster, Reprinted by permission of David Higham Associates; WALTER DE LA MARE, "The Cupboard" used by permission of The Literary Trustees of Walter de la Mare and The Society of Authors as their representative; SYDNEY FOXCROFT, article from *Sunday People*; PATSY GRAY, essay originally published in *PTA Magazine*; ELIZABETH JENNINGS, "Old Woman" from *A Sense of the World* published by André Deutsch. Reprinted by permission of David Higham Associates Ltd; NORMAN MacCAIG, "Grandchild" from *Tree of Strings.* Reprinted by permission of Chatto & Windus; HARRY MacMAHAN, "What is a Grandmother?" from *Grandmother was Quite a Girl* by Harry and Gloria MacMahan, Escondido, California; ELIZABETH MASLEN, "A Visit to Grannie" from *Treble Poets 1.* Reprinted by permission of Chatto & Windus; ANN REDPATH, excerpt from *Let this be a day for Grandparents.* Reprinted by permission of Saint Mary's Press; PENNY PERRICK, "There's no limit to the power of a granny" from *The Sun,* 9th November 1977. Reprinted by permission of London Express News and Feature Service; KUSHA PETTS, "Old Mrs Bodfan's Dance", from *Necklace for a Poor Sod.* Reprinted by permission of Gomer Press; JOHN PURSER, "In Memory of Mainie Jellett", from *The Counting Stick* © 1976, Aquila Publishing Co.: Isle of Skye; BERTRAND RUSSELL, excerpt from *The Autobiography of Bertrand Russell* published by Unwin Hyman; GEORGE SAND, extract from *Lelia, the Life of George Sand* by André Maurois. Reproduced with permission of Curtis Brown Ltd, London on behalf of The Estate of André Maurois. Copyright 1953 André Maurois; THE SUN, excerpt reprinted from *The Sun,* August 26th 1972; HILARY THOMAS, excerpt from *Grandmother Extraordinary* published by Stewart Williams Publishers. Reprinted by permission of the author; KIT WRIGHT "Babbling and Gabbling" from *Hot Dog and other Poems,* © Kit Wright, 1981. Published by Viking Kestrel and in Puffin Books. Reproduced by permission of Penguin Books Ltd.

Picture credits: A.K.G: pages 18, 24, 36, 37, 39, 48; Bridgeman Art Library: title page and pages 7, 15, 22, 27, 32, 35, 42, 44/45, 53, 54 and 55; © 1994 Charles Burleigh "A Hove Interior", page 57; © 1994 Linda Benton "Grandma's Blanket", page 7; Chris Beetles, London: cover and pages 11 and 16; City Museum & Art Gallery, Stoke-on-Trent: page 35; © Claudio Castelucho 18701927 "Spanish Dancer" page 39; Fine Art Photographic Ltd.: pages 12, 51, 57 and 61; © 1994 Wladimir Gawrilow "Junge Mütter", 1970, page 18; © 1994 Gillian Lawson "Dancing on the water III" page 32; © DACs 1994 Gimeno, Francesco "A Mother and her Daughter", 1898, page 15; Gemalde Galerie, Neue Meister, Dresden; page 48; Jeu de Paume, Paris: 59; Josef Mensing Gallery, Hamm-Rhynern page 27; © DACs 1994 Claude Monet "Un coin d'appartement", 1875, page 24; Musee d'Orsay, Paris: pages 24 and 37; Museo Omsk: page 46; Nasjonalgalleriet, Oslo: title page; Parigi, Paris: page 8; © 1994 Isa Rae "Picking Wild Flowers" page 53; Scala: pages 8, 46, 59 and 20; Skagens Museum, Denmark: page 42; Tretjakow Galerie, Moskau: pages 36 and 20; Wendy Trinder: page 31; Trustees of the Royal Watercolour Society, London: page 44/45; Whitford & Hughes, London: page 53; © 1994 E. Zampighi "Family Scene" page 27, "Her First Lesson" page 35.